First Edition
Genuine Autographed Collectible

_____
Do you want me to sign it in ink or in lipstick?

ALL YOU GET FOR NEGATIVITY IS NOTHING!
—Sharon Esther Lampert

Gift Card

Date:

To:

From:

Message

What Do Books Do?
BOOKS ARE POWERFUL!

Books Educate!
Books Enlighten!
Books Empower!
Books Emancipate!
Books Entertain!
Books Spring Eternal!
Books Drive Exploration!
Books Spark Evolution!
Books Ignite Revolution!

Sharon Esther Lampert

BooksArePowerful.com

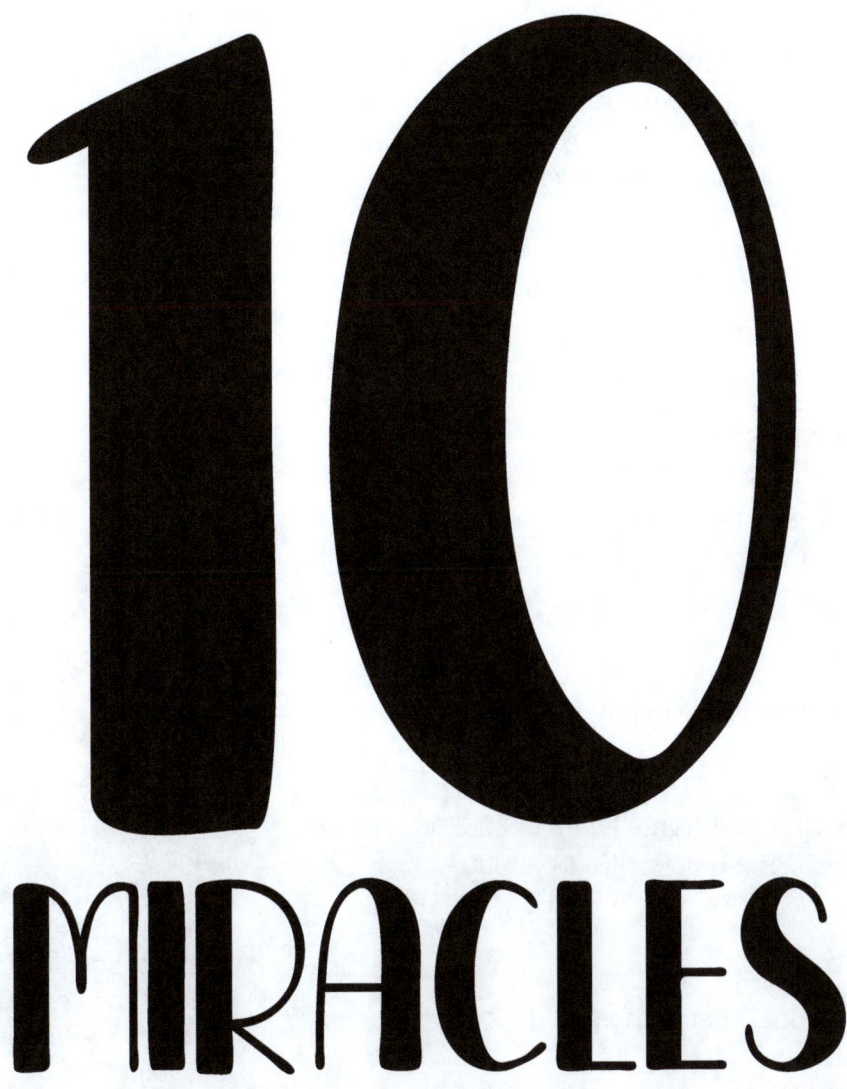

Self-Help, Mental Health, Education, Spirituality, Sharon Esther Lampert

10 MIRACLES What Happens When You Free Your Mind of Negativity?

©2024 by Sharon Esther Lampert. All Rights Reserved.
No part of this book may be used or reproduced in any manner whatsoever without written permission except in the case of brief quotations embodied in critical articles and reviews.

KADIMAH PRESS
GIFTS OF GENIUS

Books may be purchased for education, business, or sales promotional use.

ISBN Hardcover: 979-8-8690-87-73-7
ISBN Paperback: 979-8-8690-87-77-5
ISBN E-Book: 979-8-8690-87-74-4
Library of Congress Catalog Card Number: 2024900659

FAN MAIL
SharonEstherLampert.com
FANS@SharonEstherLampert.com

For Global Online Orders and Distribution:
INGRAM 1 Ingram Blvd. La Vergne, TN 37086-3629
Phone: 615-793-5000, Fax orders: 615-287-6990
Global Bookstores: USA, CAN, UK, AUS, EU, ASIA, AFRICA

Book Design and Interior:
Creatve Genius Sharon Esther Lampert
Editor: Dave Segal

First Edition

Manufactured in the United States of America

Age 9
THE QUEEN HAS ARRIVED!
"My daughter is a poet, philosopher, and teacher. She is the Princess & the Pea!
BEAUTY & BRAINS!"
MOMMY
XOXO

10 MIRACLES

What Happens When You Free Your Mind of Negativity?

KADIMAH PRESS
Gifts of Genius

DEDICATION
MOMMY
THE LOVE OF MY LIFETIME
Who Knew Who I Was From the **INSIDE OUT**!

Table of Contents

BE ART

POETREE

10 MIRACLES

Miracle 1   Choose a Fresh Start Over Dwelling in the Past ... p. 1

Miracle 2   Self-Love Over Self-Sabotage ... p. 3

Miracle 3   Facts Over Fears & Fictions ... p. 5

Miracle 4   Gratitude Over Greivances ... p. 7

Miracle 5   Calm in Storm Over Drama ... p. 9

Miracle 6   Friends Over Enemies ... p. 11

Miracle 7   Joy Over Anger ... p. 13

Miracle 8   **LIVE YOUR TRUTH** ... p. 15

Miracle 9   Helpers Over Naysayers ... p. 17

Miracle 10   Stay in Your Own Lane ... p. 19

About the Pr**odig**y ... pp. 22-24

One of the World's Greatest Poets ... p. 25

FAN MAIL ... pp. 26-31

KADIMAH PRESS: GIFTS OF GENIUS ... pp. 32-33

Count Your Blessings. Practice Gratitude. ... pp. 34-35

Sharon Esther Lampert
SEE THE WORLD THROUGH THE EYES OF A CREATIVE GENIUS

THE SOLE INTENTION OF MY POETRY
IS TO ADD LIGHT TO YOUR SOUL

FOOD IS FOR THE BODY
EDUCATION IS FOR THE MIND
POETRY IS FOR THE SOUL

LITERATURE IS POWERFUL BEYOND WORDS FOR IT CREATES WORLDS

EVERY THOUGHT IN YOUR HEAD
WAS PUT THERE BY A WRITER!

MY LIFE IS AN OPEN BOOK
TO KNOW ME IS TO READ ME

BE ART

ART IS SMART
ART IS OF THE HEART
MAKE ART NOT WAR
YOU ARE BORN FOR GREATNESS
YOU ARE A MASTERPIECE

Sharon Esther Lampert

Also by the Prodigy

The Awesome Art of Alliteration Using One Letter of The Alphabet

What Do Books Do?
—Written in Letter E

8 Goalposts of Education
—Written in Letter E

CUPID
—Written in Letter C

TEMPORARY INSANITY
We Are Building Our Lives on a Sand Trap
—Written in Letter S

PUBLISH THE SECRET SAUCE OF BOOK SALES
How to Make Money Selling Books
—Written in Letter P

NO FAKES!
NO FAT!
NO FLUFF!
NO FILLER!
NO FLOPS!
NO FUDGE!
NO F-BOMB!

DESTINY
Are You Living Your Life By Default or by Design?
—Written in Letter D

POWER
—Written in Letter P

THERAPY
—Written in Letter T

POETREE

Ink needs a Pen
Pen needs Paper
Paper needs a Poem
Poem needs a Poet
Poet needs a Muse
Muse needs a Poet
Poet needs Divine Inspiration
Divine Inspiration needs Divine Intervention
Divine Intervention needs Divine Grace
Divine Grace needs Immortality
Immortality needs Eternity
Eternity needs Readers of Poetry

By Sharon Esther Lampert

@All Rights Reserved. Sharon Esther Lampert.

POWER Mantra

Follow Your Passion
Fulfill Your Potential
Find Your Place In The World

Passion & Purpose
Potential & Possibility
Plan in Place on Paper
Priorities and Preparation
Positive, Patience & Perseverance
Productivity & Progress
Prosperity

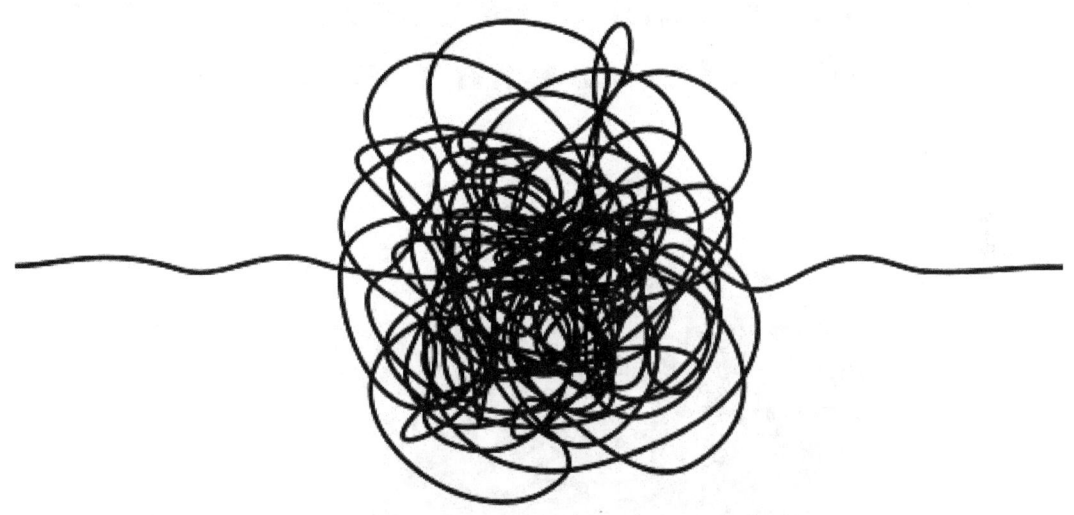

"There are millions of people in this world who are tortured by their own minds."

– Ekhart Tolle

NEGATIVITY of PAST MISTAKES

You Cannot Right the Wrongs of the Past!
Make Peace with Your Past!

10 MIRACLES

What Happens When You Free Your Mind of Negativity?

Miracle I

Choose a Fresh Start!

**Enjoy a Brand New Day
Full of Unlimited Possibility**

**Forget the MISTAKE
Remember the LESSON**

I'm allowed to make mistakes, and
I'm allowed to learn from my mistakes.

Sharon Esther Lampert

NEGATIVITY of INNER CRITICS
Free Yourself of Uninterupted Self-Criticism
Stop Beating Up on Yourself and Others

What Happens When You Free Your Mind of Negativity?

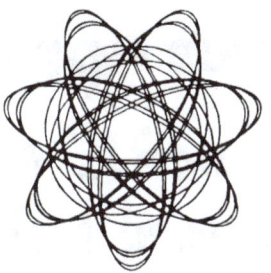

Miracle 2
No More Self-Sabotage

Transform Negative Self-Talk into Positive Self-Talk

Transform Self-Hatred into Self-Love

The Most Important Relationship is the One You Have with Yourself.

Love Yourself Unconditionally!

Transform "I'm Not Good Enough" into "I'm More Than Enough and Worthy of Self Respect and Self-Love."

Sharon Esther Lampert

NEGATIVITY of FEAR
ANALYSIS PARALYSIS

False Evidence Appearing Real

The Choice Is Yours:
Fear: Face Everything and Run
Fear: Face Everything and Rise

What Happens When You Free Your Mind of Negativity?

Miracle 3

Focus on Facts Not Fears
Focus on Facts Not Fictions

Transform Information into Knowledge and Knowledge into Wisdom

Transform Fear into Fierce!

NEGATIVITY of SELF-PITY

Life Is Unfair! Life Owes You Nothing! Stop Whining, Moaning, Griping, Complaining, Beefing, and Self-Pity: "Woe Is Me!"

What Happens When You Free Your Mind of Negativity?

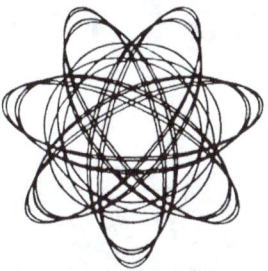

Miracle 4
Count Your Blessings

Gratitude over Grievances!

Practice Daily Gratitude

Don't Take Anything or Anyone for Granted!

NEGATIVITY of Chronic Stress
Worry, Anxiety, Stress, Depression, and PTSD

What Happens When You Free Your Mind of Negativity?

Miracle 5
Become the Calm in a Storm
Practice Inner Peace

- Practice Meditation
- Practice Mindfulness
- Find a Daily Mantra
- Listen to Beautiful Music

"Meditation, Mindfulness, and Music Mitigates Madness"
— Sharon Esther Lampert

NEGATIVITY of HATE SPEECH

**Stop Behind the Back Bashing!
Stop Throwing People Under the Bus!
Stop Abusing Family, Friends, and
Strangers at Home, at Work and on
Social Media with Hate.**

What Happens When You Free Your Mind of Negativity?

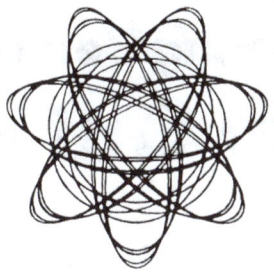

Miracle 6
Make Friends Not Enemies
Rebuild Your Personal and Professional Relationships
"Thank you for sharing!"
Practice Tolerance, Understanding, Empathy Respect, and Love!

NEGATIVITY of ANGER

Life Is a Rollar Coaster Ride of Highs and Lows Stuff May Go Wrong Before It Goes Right!
Don't Lash Out in Anger!

What Happens When You Free Your Mind of Negativity?

Miracle 7
Exhale Anger! Inhale Joy!

To Achieve Goals, Practice (1) Patience (2) Positive and (3) Perserverance

Divide and Conquer! Take Baby Steps!

One Foot in Front of the Other!

Sharon Esther Lampert

NEGATIVITY of CHILDHOOD CONDITIONING

Habitual Patterns of Behavior Indoctrinated in Childhood May No Longer Serve You: Religious, Cultural, and Social

What Happens When You Free Your Mind of Negativity?

Miracle 8
LIVE YOUR TRUTH!
Think Your Own Thoughts!
Listen to Your Own Voice!

Sharon Esther Lampert

NEGATIVITY of SELF-HARM

Quit Harmful Addictive Behaviors
Abusing Food, Alcohol or Drugs
Toxic Relationships
Risky, Aggressive or Excessive Behaviors

All People Help You with Their Strengths and Hurt You with Their Weaknesses

— Sharon Esther Lampert

10 MIRACLES

What Happens When You Free Your Mind of Negativity?

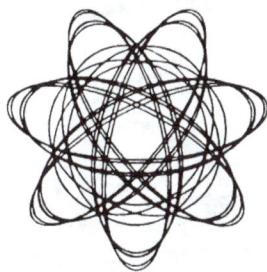

Miracle 9
Find the Helpers!
Seek Out Professional Help
Implement a Success Strategy

*"Good People, Nothing is a Problem
Bad People, Everything is a Problem"*
— Sharon Esther Lampert

NEGATIVITY of LIVING LIFE on SOMEONE ELSE'S TERMS
Only You Know What's Best for You!

10 MIRACLES

What Happens When You Free Your Mind of Negativity?

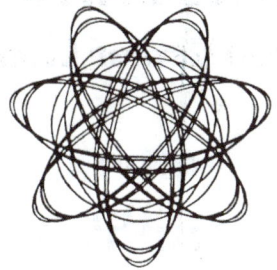

Miracle 10
Stay in Your Own Lane
Everyone Is On a Different Journey

Don't Get Sidetracked into Someone Else's Life Story!

"Follow Your Passion, Fulfill Your Potential and Find Your Place in the World!"
—Sharon Esther Lampert

Meditation, Mindfulness, and Music Mitigates Madness
— Sharon Esther Lampert

ALL YOU GET FOR NEGATIVITY IS NOTHING!
—Sharon Esther Lampert

Good People, Nothing Is a Problem
Bad People, Everything Is a Problem
—Sharon Esther Lampert

All People Help You with Their Strenghs and Hurt You with Their Weaknesses
— Sharon Esther Lampert

Follow Your Passion
Fulfill Your Potential
Find Your Place in the World
— Sharon Esther Lampert

10 MIRACLES

HAPPINESS IS AN ACT OF DEFIANCE
Sharon Esther Lampert

Sharon Esther Lampert

Poet
Philosopher
Peacemaker
Prophet
Princess & **P**ea
PIN-UP
Performer: Vocalist
Player: Jock
Paladin of Education:
PHOTON SUPERHERO
Princess Kadimah
President
Publisher
Producer: FILMMAKER
Psychobiologist
Piano-**P**laying Cat
Phoenix
Prodigy

NYU
Honored Sharon Lampert with an Award for *"Multi-Interdisciplinary Studies"*

Websites:
SharonEstherLampert.com
PhilosopherQueen.com
WorldFamousPoems.com
PoetryJewels.com
Schmaltzy.com
GodIsGoDo.com
TrueLoveBurnsEternal.com
SillyLittleBoys.com
WinAtThin.com
HappyGrandparenting.com
BooksArePowerful.com
WomenHaveAllThePower.com
WritersRuntheWorld.com

PUBLISHER
PalmBeachBookPublisher.com
MiamiBookPublisher.com

EDUCATION
Smartgrades.com
EverydayanEasyA.com
BooksnotBombs.com
PhotonSuperhero.com

10 MIRACLES
About the Prodigy

Sharon Esther Lampert
Gifted: Born with an Extra-Body Part: "Creative Apparatus"

Prodigy — Princess and the Pea!
Unleash the Creator the God Within: 10 Esoteric Laws of Genius and Creativity

Poet — One of the World's Greatest Poets
POETRY WORLD RECORD: 120 WORDS OF RHYME
The Greatest Poems Ever Written on Extraordinary World Events
http://famouspoetsandpoems.com/poets.html

Philosopher Queen
- TEMPORARY INSANITY: We Are Building Our Lives on a Sand Trap — Written in Letter S
- God of What? 11 Esoteric Laws of Inextricability Is Life a Gift or a Punishment?

Prophet
- 22 COMMANDMENTS: All You Will Ever Need to Know About God
- WHO KNEW GOD WAS SUCH A CHATTERBOX — **GOD IS GO! DO!**

Peacemaker
WORLD PEACE EQUATION

PALADIN OF EDUCATION
SMARTGRADES BRAIN POWER REVOLUTION
- The Silent Crisis Destroying America's Brightest Minds — BOOK OF THE MONTH!
- EVERY DAY AN EASY A!   everydayaneasya.com

Pioneer
- Silly Little Boys: 40 Rules of Manhood
- CUPID: The Language of Love — Written in Letter C
- PUBLISH: The Secret Sauce of Book Sales — Written in Letter P
- Love You More Than Yesterday: 14 Relationship Strategies for Happily Ever After
- WIN AT THIN: Fat Me, Skinny Me

Princess Kadimah
8TH PROPHETESS OF ISRAEL: THE 22 COMMANDMENTS

PIN-UP
SEXIEST CREATIVE GENIUS IN HUMAN HISTORY

Sharon Esther Lampert

Artists March to the Beat of a Different Drummer
Sharon Esther Lampert Marches to the Beat of an Entire Orchestra

**Poet, Philosopher, Prophet, Peacemaker
Paladin of Education, Princess & Pea
Phoenix, PHOTON, PINUP, Prodigy**

Blue-Eyed. Brilliant. Beautiful. Buxom. Books. Blessed.

Sharon Esther Lampert was born an OLD SOUL — She was never young! Sharon is a lefty.

At age nine, her mother declared: "My daughter is a poet, philosopher, and teacher!" She nicknamed her daughter, "The Princess and the Pea!"

Sharon's greatest literary works woke her up in the middle of the night — and made her get up out of bed — and write them down. Sharon writes an entire book in one day!

Sharon's mother was the sole person in Sharon's life who knew who she was from the inside out — and what would become of her. Her beloved mother also knew to her very last breath... the exact day and to the minute when she would die! (Eve Paikoff Lampert: June 3, 1925 — May 5, 1985).

Later in life, Sharon will purchase a green-pea pendant, at the Broadway show, "Once Upon a Mattress" starring Sarah Jessica Parker. She wore the green pea every day around her neck with a beautiful Jewish-star pendant purchased in Haifa, Israel at age 16.

Sharon Esther's Gifts Are Metaphysical — Beyond the Scope of Scientific Inquiry

There Are No Rough Drafts! — The Books Write Themselves!
(There Are 4 Books with God in the Title)

"A LIST" Sharon Esther Lampert is One of the World's Greatest Poets
http://famouspoetsandpoems.com/poets.html

#1 Poetry Website for Student Projects

On a global scale, Sharon's poetry is used by teachers for their poetry lesson plans, and by students for their poetry school projects.

New York University Awards — (YOUTUBE Videos)

Sharon Esther earned three degrees from NYU — and she was honored with two NYU awards. Sharon represented her class at her graduation — and was honored with an award for "Multi-Interdisciplinary Studies." She also played on the NYU Women's Varsity Basketball Team as a center in the $16-million Coles Sports Center. Sharon won an "NYU Weightlifting Contest" — Sharon was the sole contestant — so she won! (NYU newspaper article).

10 MIRACLES
One of the World's Greatest Poets

 Amy Levy (69)
(1861 - 1889)

 Louise Labe (1)
(1524 - 1566)

 David Lehman (58)
(1948 - present)

 Jiri Mordecai Langer (1)
(1894 - 1943)

 John Lindley (4)
(1952 - present)

 Dimitris Lyacos (3)
(1966 - present)

 Yahia Lababidi (10)
(1973 - present)

 Walter Savage Landor (52)
(1775 - 1864)

 Michael Lally (1)
(1942 - present)

 Major Henry Livingston, Jr. (23)
(1748 - 1828)

 Roddy Lumsden (2)
(1966 - present)

 Sharmagne Leland-St. John (5)
(1953 - present)

 Sharon Esther Lampert (19)
(0 - present)

M

 Claude McKay (76)
(1889 - 1948)

 Spike Milligan (35)
(1918 - 2002)

 Marianne Moore (18)
(1887 - 1972)

 John Milton (102)
(1608 - 1674)

 A. A. Milne (22)
(1882 - 1956)

 Czeslaw Milosz (33)
(1911 - 2004)

 Roger McGough (14)
(1937 - present)

 Walter de la Mare (44)
(1873 - 1956)

 Antonio Machado (8)
(1875 - 1939)

 Edna St. Vincent Millay (165)
(1892 - 1950)

 W. S. Merwin (23)
(1927 - present)

 John Masefield (25)
(1878 - 1967)

Sharon Esther Lampert

FAN MAIL
FANS@SharonEstherLampert.com

Ardent Fan and Admirer Harry McVeety
A PHENOMENON ...
SHARON ESTHER LAMPERT

Lithe and lovely ... like a fawn.
This lady fascinates me ... from dusk till dawn.
Feminine and comely ... she's beyond belief
A blue-beam from her eyes ... is my soothing relief.

Girlish in her braces ... maidenly in her style
I yearn for her embraces ... and adore her friendly smile.
As tasteful as any artist ... you'll ever see
She's a compendium of class ... from A to Z.

If you'd like to see a figure, that puts Venus to shame
Behold her in a swimsuit, and your passions will aflame.
Ever exuding goodness . . . guided from above
Miss Sharon is the essence, and epitome of Love.

She's the inspiration of sages, and also fools like me
And the most magnificent female, I'm sure I'll ever see.
The nights are now endearing, & never filled with doubt
I sometimes wake up singing, cause it's Sharon . . .
I dream about.

Affectionately,. .
A devoted fan,
—Harry McVeety

10 MIRACLES

FAN MAIL
FANS@SharonEstherLampert.com

Sharon Esther Lampert

FAN MAIL
FANS@SharonEstherLampert.com

Congregation Emanu-El
of the City of New York
Fifth Avenue at Sixty-fifth Street
New York, N.Y. 10021-6596

Study of
DAVID M. POSNER

September 22, 1999

The New York Public Library
Humanities and Social Sciences Library
Fifth Avenue and 42nd Street
New York, NY 10018-2788

Dear Friends:

  Sharon Esther Lampert has made application for a fellowship from the Center for Scholars and Writers. It is with greatest pleasure that I write to you in support of her application.

  I can best describe this remarkable woman by citing the analysis of Moses Maimonides, in his "Guide for the Perplexed," concerning psychological endowments. He noted the class of people who are intellectually superior, but whose imaginative faculties are deficient. These, he said, were philosophers. Then there are those whose imaginative faculties are highly developed, but who are deficient intellectually. He said these are dreamers and politicians. But then he observed the rare people who have both highly developed intellects and imaginations. These, he said, are prophets.

  Sharon Esther Lampert falls into the last category. She has one of the most gifted intellects I have ever encountered, and her imaginative capacity is absolutely awesome.

  I have known many people throughout my long career at Temple Emanu-El. I have never met anyone like this extraordinary human being.

  Again, awesome is the most appropriate word.

Yours truly,

[signature]

FORMED BY THE CONSOLIDATION OF EMANU-EL CONGREGATION AND TEMPLE BETH-EL

10 MIRACLES

FAN MAIL
FANS@SharonEstherLampert.com

Ardent Fan and Admirer Felix Fojas

Dear Sharon,

You are not only an exquisite poet, you're beautiful! Am smitten by your luminous beingness. Are you an angel in disguise--a so-called malachim in Hebrew if I am not mistaken.

Thank you for your wondeful open-hearted response.

Your photo will sit next to those of Gautama Buddha and the Blessed Virgin Mary.

I will follow your sound esoteric advise regarding the positioning of your photo and the two other icons.

I am deeply impressed that you are very conscious about the concept of sacred space and the flow of spiritual energy.

So please send me your precious photo as soon as possible.

P.S. Will you be generous enough to send me your signed photo which I will place on the secret altar of my heart, lit by the menorah, the seven-stemmed candelabra of your inspiration, O mystical muse, O Rose of Sharon...

Your ardent fan and admirer,

—Felix Fojas, the cybercat with a mystical meow
Chico, CA, 95926

Sharon Esther Lampert

FAN MAIL
FANS@SharonEstherLampert.com

December 2001

Dear Kadimah:
You are truly a remarkable woman. You are a wonderful word-weaver. You are great in spirit and inspire everyone. You have insights on multiple things. You "see" while others stumble along.

That is why you bear the Light. That is why you cry out for Hope in the midst of despair. That is why you are always a step away from the multitude, yet when you speak they cry,

"She is our voice and says what we have felt all the time."

Blessed are those who have you for a friend.
Sincerely,
—Reverend Aaron R. Orr
Hamilton, Ontario, Canada
http://owensinc.freeyellow.com

WHO AM I?
My Name is Aaron Robin Orr and I was born in Belfast, Northern Ireland on November 16, 1940 the only son of Andrew Orr and Hessie Orr. They were Presbyterian by denomination and Christian by life and practice. In September 1965 I married my wife, the former Ruth Hannah Hawkins and never has a man been more blessed than I. We have two children, Elizabeth and Andrew. Beth is married to our son-in-law Remo Pace, gave us our first granddaughter Rachael almost two years ago. Andrew is still single and is involved in various endeavours one of which is writing for an Internet magazine.

10 MIRACLES
FAN MAIL
FANS@SharonEstherLampert.com

November 30 2005
Hello Sharon,
Here are my thoughts on your work.
Poetry is a reflection of the spirit and Sharon Esther Lampert with every breath and every word fulfills her souls purpose.
Her words dance as flowers in the wind.
Life is to be celebrated and Sharon provides those blessed to be touched by her work a world of harmony and joy that is delightful and memorable.
The LIGHT within her shines in her work and enriches and enlightens the reader. There is a beauty to the truth of her poetry that is breathtaking.
I am honoured to have crossed paths with one so gifted.
Sharons poetry connects the reader to the infinite flowing source of life.
She is a spiritual seeker that is connected to the divine.
Her work is authentic and effective, a mirror to the soul that is thought provoking and inspiring.
I am blessed to have read her words for they are a vibrant tapestry that opens the heart and nourishes the spirit.
Every word she writes is woven of DIVINE LIGHT and has within it the knowledge of a thousand winds.
Sharon Esther Lampert is a messenger of hope whose many gifts plant new seeds and cultivate a greater appreciation for life and all its beauty.
She has provided a body of work that is rich with profound truths. Raw and beautiful, sensitive and radiating with positive energy,
Sharon ventures down an enlightened path and generously takes us with her.
I am a better man today for having read her spiritually illuminating words.
May the whispers of her soul awaken a healing light that illuminates a playground for transformation and a kingdom of infinite possibilities.
Have a beautiful day.
—**Micheal Teal**
The Ancient One

Sharon Esther Lampert

KADIMAH PRESS: GIFTS OF GENIUS

Poet: The Greatest Poems Ever Written on Extraordinary World Events
Title: I Stole All the Words from the Dictionary

ISBN Hardcover: 978-1-885872-06-7
ISBN Paperback: 978-1-885872-07-4
ISBN E-Book: 978-1-885872-08-1

Prophet: WORLD PREMIERE!
Title: WHO KNEW GOD WAS SUCH A CHATTERBOX

ISBN Hardcover: 978-1-885872-33-3
ISBN Paperback: 978-1-885872-34-0
ISBN E-Book: 978-1-885872-36-4

Prophet: WORLD PREMIERE!
A Universal Moral Compass For All Religions, For All People, For All Time
Title: The 22 Commandments: All You Will Ever Need to know About GOD

ISBN Hardcover: 978-1-885872-03-6
ISBN Paperback: 978-1-885872-04-3
ISBN E-Book: 978-1-885872-05-0

Philosopher: WORLD PREMIERE!
Title: God of What? 11 Esoteric Laws of Inextricability

ISBN Hardcover: 978-1-885872-00-5
ISBN Paperback: 978-1-885872-01-2
ISBN E-Book: 978-1-885872-02-9
GodofWhat.com

NO FAKES!
NO FAT!
NO FLUFF!
NO FILLER!
NO FLOPS!
NO FUDGE!
NO FBOMB!

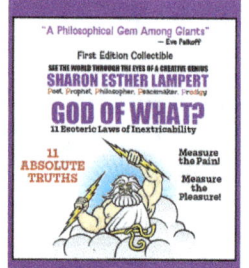

Prodigy: WORLD PREMIERE!
Title: Unleash the Creator The God Within: 10 Esoteric Laws of Genius and

ISBN Hardcover: 978-1-885872-21-0
ISBN Paperback: 978-1-885872-22-7
ISBN E-Book: 978-1-885872-23-4

10 MIRACLES

KADIMAH PRESS: GIFTS OF GENIUS

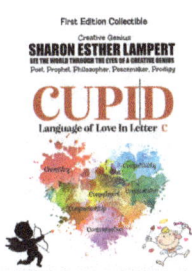

Prodigy: WORLD PREMIERE!
Title: CUPID: The Language of Love — Written in Letter C
ISBN Hardcover: 978-1-885872-55-5
ISBN Paperback: 978-1-885872-56-2
ISBN E-Book: 978-1-885872-57-9
SharonEstherLampert.com

Popular: Children's Book — True Story of a Piano-Playing Cat
Title: SCHMALTZY: In America, Even a Cat Can Have a Dream
ISBN Hardcover: 978-1-885872-39-5
ISBN Paperback: 978-1-885872-38-8
ISBN E-Book: 978-1-885872-37-1
Schmaltzy.com

Popular: WORLD PREMIERE!
Title: SILLY LITTLE BOYS: 40 RULES OF MANHOOD
How Do Silly Little Boys Grow into Big Sane Men?
For Men of All Ages — 14 Global Catastrophes of Violence Against Women
ISBN Hardcover: 978-1-885872-29-6
ISBN Paperback: 978-1-885872-35-7
ISBN E-Book: 978-1-885872-41-8
SillyLittleBoys.com

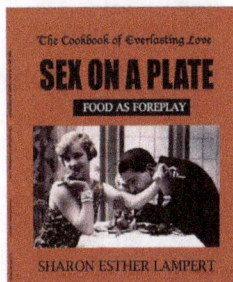

Popular: Every Great Relationship Begins with the Perfect Meal
Title: SEX ON A PLATE: FOOD AS FOREPLAY
The Cookbook of Everlasting Love
ISBN Hardcover: 978-1-885872-46-3
ISBN Paperback: 978-1-885872-48-7
ISBN E-Book: 978-1-885872-47-0
TrueLoveBurnsEternal.com

Sharon Esther Lampert

Count Your Blessings. Practice Gratitude.

Blessing 1. Genetics & Gift of Genius — Lefty
- Genetic Inheritance: Painter Grandfather Benjamin Paikoff & Sculptor Father Abraham Lampert
- Vocalist: Estelle Leibling, Chaim Frieberg, Ashira Orchestra, 18 Years: Ramaz Women's Service (YOUTUBE)
- Athlete: "Faster Than Any Boy, Anytime, Anywhere, Any Age!"

Blessing 2. My Life: Dawn of the Digital Revolution
- APPLE: The Golden Age of Personal Computers
- ADOBE: The Golden Age of Creativity
- INGRAM: The Golden Age of Publishing
- SOCIAL MEDIA: The Golden Age of the Internet & Global Communication
- iTUNES: The Golden Age of Music & Lyrics

Blessing 3. My Loved Ones
- Self-Love
- Unconditional True Love: Mommy Eve Lampert
- My PURRfect Children: SCHMALTZY and FALAFEL (Schmaltzy.com)
- My Metaphysical Sister: Poet Hannah Szenses: "ELI, ELI"
- My MUSE: Karl Bardosh "Friends First and Forever, and Family"
- My Boyfriends, Muses, and Playdates (NYC Night Life: Broadway Shows, Concerts, Restaurants)
- My Bubbe Esther Tulkoff (EstherTulkoff.com)

Blessing 4. My Education, Educators and Awards
- NYU BA, MA, MA and NYU Award for Multi-Interdisciplinary Studies (YouTube videos)
- NYU Professor Laurin Raiken and MA Class Representative at Graduation
- NYC Rockefeller University, Publication: "Hyperphagia and Obesity Induced by Neuropeptide Y" — Lab of Dr. Sarah Leibowitz and Dr. Glen Stanley
- NYC 100-Year Scholarship Award Winner, Presented by NYC Mayor Edward Koch
- NY Empire Science Scholarship Award Winner
- Jerusalem Fellowship Award, Aish Hatorah, Israel
- First Prize: Upper East Side Resident Writing Contest
- First Prize: First Prize WAVE Newspaper Art Contest

Blessing 5. My Sports
- NYC Marathon
- Basketball: NYU Women's Varsity Basketball Team, Center
- Basketball: NYC Urban Professional League
- Skiing: Heavenly, Lake Tahoe, Nevada
- Tennis: NYC Central Park Tennis Courts
- NYU Weightlifting Contest Winner! NYU Coles Sports Center (I was the only contestant — so I won!)
- Coach Sandy Pyonin: Basketball and Softball
- Coaches: Chicago Bulls Phil Jackson and Boston Celtics Bill Walton, Omega Institute, NY

Blessing 6. My Inspirations
- ISRAEL: "AM YISRAEL CHAI!" (Lambs to Slaughter to LIONS to Light of the World — 22% of Nobel Prizes)
- NYC: The Golden Age of Personal Freedom & Self-Expression
- America: Land of Possibility, Potential, and Promise

10 MIRACLES

NYU Professor **Laurin Raiken** and Me at My Graduation

NYU Professor **Karl Bardosh** and Me Friend & Family

NYU President **Andrew Hamilton** and Me, Boca Raton, Florida

NYU President **L.J. Olivia** and Me Class Representative at Graduation

I Am Mortal.
My Books Are Immortal.
My Books Are My Remains.
Please Handle Them Gently!

This book was compiled in 3 parts:
Part 1. BIRTH — January 27, 2021
Part 2. Format Book — July 2022
Part 3. Publish Book — January 2024

Sharon Esther Lampert
SEE THE WORLD THROUGH THE EYES OF A CREATIVE GENIUS
Poet, Philosopher, Prophet, Peacemaker, Princess & Pea, Prodigy

www.ingramcontent.com/pod-product-compliance
Lightning Source LLC
LaVergne TN
LVHW081315060526
838201LV00005B/170